know your pet

CATS

Anna and Michael Sproule

The Bookwright Press
New York · 1988

636.8
5

Know Your Pet

Cats
Dogs
Hamsters
Rabbits

First published in the
United States in 1988 by
The Bookwright Press
387 Park Avenue South
New York. NY 10016

First published in 1988 by
Wayland (Publishers) Limited,
61 Western Road, Hove,
East Sussex, BN3 1JD, England.

© BLA Publishing Limited 1988

Library of Congress Cataloging in Publication Data

Sproule, Anna
  Know your pet cat.

  Bibliography: p.
  Includes index .
  Summary: Discusses how to choose and care for a
pet cat, with information on various breeds.
   1. Cats — Juvenile literature. 2. Cat breeds —
Juvenile literature. [1.Cats. 2. Cat breeds]
I. Sproule, Michael   II. Title
SF445.7.S67   1988   636.8   87-34142
ISBN 0-531-18214-2

Designed and produced by BLA Publishing
Limited, East Grinstead, Sussex, England.

A member of the Ling Kee Group
LONDON · HONG KONG · TAIPEI · SINGAPORE · NEW YORK

Photographic credits

t = top, b = bottom, l = left, r = right

cover: Chris Fairclough Picture Library

8 Animals Unlimited; 9t ZEFA; 9b, 10 Chris
Fairclough Picture Library; 11 Animals Unlimited;
12t Anthony Bannister/NHPA; 12b Jonathan
Scott/Seaphot; 14t Camilla Jessel Photo Library; 14b
Trevor Hill; 16 Michael Holford; 17 DeWynters; 18,
19 Animals Unlimited; 21t D.N. Dalton/NHPA; 21b
Vision International; 22, 23, 24, 25t Animals
Unlimited; 25b ZEFA; 26 Animals Unlimited; 28, 29t
Chris Fairclough Picture Library; 29b D.N.
Dalton/NHPA; 30t Chris Fairclough Picture Library;
30b Geoscience Features; 32l Elizabeth Gabriel; 32r
Trevor Hill; 34t Chris Fairclough Picture Library;
34b, 35t, 35b Animals Unlimited; 36t Chris
Fairclough Picture Library; 36b Spectrum Colour
Library; 38, 39 Animals Unlimited; 40t Mansell
Collection; 40b Chris Fairclough Picture Library; 42t
Animals Unlimited; 42b, 43t Lacz Lemoine/NHPA;
43b Animals Unlimited

Editorial planning by Jollands Editions
Color origination by Waterden Reproductions
Illustrations by Derick Bown/Linden Artists;
Steve Lings/Linden Artists; and Clive Spong/
Linden Artists
Printed in Italy by G. Canale & C.S.p.A. – Turin

Cover: Although generally independent by nature, all cats from the aristocratic pedigreed to the domestic tabby pictured here require a lot of time, care and affection.

Title page: In typical cat fashion, this ginger tabby has sought out a warm, comfortable place to sit.

Contents

Note to the Reader

In this book there are some words in the text that are printed in **bold** type. This shows that the word is listed in the glossary on page 44. The glossary gives a brief explanation of words that may be new to you.

Introduction

A cat is part of the family in one out of every five homes in the United States, Britain and Canada. In France and Australia even more people have cats. In those countries one out of every three homes has a cat for a pet. Why is it that so many people like to have a cat in the home?

Keeping a cat

Cats are easy to have around and their food is not expensive. They are quiet and peaceful animals and do not seem to need very much attention. For people who live alone, a cat can be a good companion. If you have a cat in your home you will not be troubled by mice. Some people keep cats for this reason alone.

▼ When kittens are a few weeks old, they become very lively. They may be fun to look at, but five is too many for most homes! Now is the time to find new homes for some of them.

▶ All cats from the humblest domestic to the aristocratic Persian pictured here are creatures of comfort. They enjoy nothing more than curling up on the rug in front of the fire, or taking over your favorite armchair.

▼ A cat likes to be touched gently and petted by its owner. Look at the expression on this tabby's face. You can tell by the closed eyes that the cat is happy and peaceful. Most cats also purr when they are pleased.

In return, your cat will depend on you for food, shelter, affection and good health. This means that you will need to devote some time to your cat every day. Think very carefully before you make up your mind to have a cat, or any other pet for that matter. You must be very sure that you can spare the time and money to be a good, caring owner for the rest of the animal's life.

Becoming a cat-owner

Before you decide to become a cat-owner, make sure that everyone in your home thinks that it is a good idea. Will your new pet be welcomed and loved by the whole family?

If you want to, you can buy an expensive kitten from a pet shop or a **breeder**. But you do not have to do this. Kittens or full-grown cats can often be obtained free, or at very little cost. Perhaps you know a cat-owner who has a spare kitten needing a good home. There are also animal shelters, like the ASPCA, that take in unwanted kittens and stray cats. They are looking for people like you all the time. But they will want to be sure that you will know how to treat your cat and look after it.

9

How to choose your cat

If you have not kept a cat before, you should think carefully before you decide to have one. First find out as much as you can about cats. This book will help you, but you should also read other books. Talk to any of your friends or relatives who own cats. They should be able to give you some useful advice.

If you get the chance, go to a cat show and have a good look around. You will be surprised to see how many different kinds of cats there are.

Different cats

At a cat show you will find that the cats are divided into two groups, **pedigreed** and **domestic**. Pedigreed cats have parents and ancestors of the same breed and are more expensive to buy. Domestic cats have parents from mixed breeds.

Cats are also divided in another way— longhair and shorthair. Longhairs take up more of their owner's time because they need to be **groomed**—that is brushed and combed—each day. Shorthairs take less time to groom than longhairs, and do not need to be groomed so often.

A kitten should be at least ten weeks old before it leaves its mother. Cats usually have three or four kittens at a time. Almost all kittens look attractive, but study them all closely before you choose one from a **litter**. Which one seems the most lively? Does one of them come toward you in a friendly way? Do not choose a kitten with sore, weeping eyes or a runny nose. Take someone with you to the pet shop or ASPCA who knows about cats and can help you make your choice. The most important thing is to take plenty of time making your choice.

▼ An animal shelter, such as the ASPCA, looks after unwanted animals, and strays that have been brought in off the street. You could obtain your cat from one of these places for a small amount of money. As you can see in this picture, there are cats of all kinds to choose from.

► It is fun to visit a cat show if you are able to do so. Here each cat is shown in a separate cage. This will give you a chance to decide what breed of cat you would like to have as your own pet.

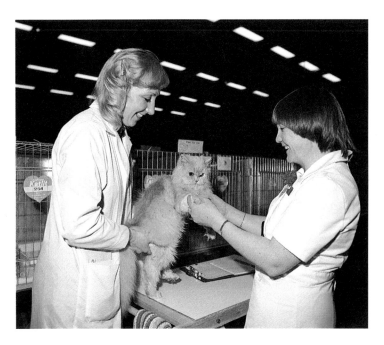

The older cat

If you decide to start off with an **adult** cat, you need to be extra cautious in making your decision. It may not have been well cared for in its first home. Stray cats are sometimes vicious, and may bite or scratch strangers. In any case, it is important to take any new cat to a vet. The vet will check its health and tell you if it has any weaknesses.

Which cat is for me?

Kitten or adult?

Male or female?

What color?

Longhair or shorthair?

Large or small?

Pedigreed or domestic?

The cat family

Domestic cats belong to a large group of animals called the cat family. Lions and tigers are big cats, so are leopards and cheetahs. Members of the cat family all behave in similar ways. Sometimes, if you look at your pet cat, you can see it behaving like a small tiger or a small leopard.

Cats as hunters

Cats are **carnivores**, or meat eaters. In the wild, they live on the flesh of other animals, which they hunt and kill. They use their sharp claws to catch their victims, and their four long, pointed **canine teeth** to bite into the flesh. All cats except cheetahs have claws that they can draw back inside their toes. They draw in their claws when running, and bring them out for the kill or for climbing trees. Cats also bring their claws out when they are angry—so be careful.

In the wild, cats hunt mainly by night. It is often said they can see in the dark. This is not quite true. But cats can certainly see very well when there is only a little light. The **pupils** of their eyes open wide to make the most of what light there is.

Watch your cat

Kittens are born with the **instinct** to hunt, and are taught the skills by their mothers. Even pet cats that are well fed need to hunt if they are to live full, contented lives. Often cats pretend to be hunting. It is a kind of game for them. Watch a cat when it is outdoors, when there are leaves blowing around in a breeze. When a cat sees a movement, it may sit still for a very long time, waiting for the moment to attack. It will measure the distance carefully, and then pounce.

▲ The serval is a small cat that is found in parts of Africa. As you can see from its two canine teeth, this cat is very fierce.

▼ The big cats are master hunters. This East African lion is just about to pounce on some unwary prey. If you watch your pet cat at play or when it is stalking a bird or mouse, you will often see it take up this typical hunting position.

▲ The center part of the eye is called the pupil. At night, cats open the pupil wide and can see quite well. In sunlight, the pupil becomes a narrow slit.

Cats have many other skills to help them. They have a good sense of balance and are sure-footed. Cats can climb quickly up trees, using their claws and their powerful hind legs. They can drop from a height, always landing safely on their feet. Cats have all the skills needed for hunting and for living in the wild.

The cat family

Name	Typical weight kg (lb)	Habitat	Colour
Big cats			
Cheetah	40 (88)	Africa, Middle East, South Asia	Sandy, dark spots
Clouded leopard	50 (110)	South and southeast Asia	Pale brown, darker mottles
Jaguar	90 (198)	Central America	Yellow-brown, spots in clusters, or dark brown
Leopard	55 (121)	Africa, South Asia	Pale brown, darker spots or dark brown
Lion	200 (441)	Southern Africa and India	Sandy brown
Snow leopard	50 (110)	Central Asia	Light gray, darker spots
Tiger	250 (551)	South and southeast Asia	Orange with black stripes
Small cats			
African golden cat	15 (38)	West and central Africa	Brown and gray
Asiatic golden cat	8 (18)	Eastern Asia	Golden brown
Bay cat	3 (7)	Borneo	Bright reddish brown
Black-footed cat	2 (4)	Southern Africa	Light brown, dark patches
Bobcat	10 (22)	North America	Reddish brown, dark spots
Caracal	20 (44)	Africa, Arabia, North India	Reddish brown to yellow gray
Chinese desert cat	5 (11)	Mongolia, China	Yellow-brown, dark broken stripes
Fishing cat	8 (18)	South and southeast Asia	Sandy with dark spots
Flat-headed cat	7 (15)	Southeast Asia	Reddish brown
Geoffroy's cat	3 (7)	South America	Gray or sandy, dark spots
Iriomote cat	5 (11)	Taiwan	Sandy with dark spots
Jaguarundi	10 (22)	Southern U.S., Central and South America	Red or gray
Jungle cat	10 (22)	Egypt, southern Asia	Sandy brown, ringed tail
Kodkod	3 (7)	South America	Gray, dark spots
Leopard cat	5 (11)	Southeast Asia	Yellow with black spots
Lynx	20 (44)	Europe, North America, northern Asia	Light brown, dark spots
Marbled cat	5 (11)	Southeast Asia	Sandy with dark patches
Margay cat	6 (13)	Central and South America	Yellow brown, dark spots
Mountain cat	5 (11)	South America	Brown to gray, dark spots
Ocelot	12 (26)	Southern U.S., South America	Yellow or gray, dark spots and stripes
Pallas's cat	4 (9)	Central Asia	Orange gray, black and white head markings
Pampas cat	5 (11)	South America	Gray with dark spots
Puma	50 (110)	North and South America	Varies from sandy to black
Rusty-spotted cat	2 (4)	South India and Sri Lanka	Red with brown patches
Sand cat	2 (4)	North Africa, Middle East, southwest Asia	Sandy to gray brown, tail ringed
Serval	14 (31)	Africa	Sandy with dark spots
Tiger cat	3 (7)	Central and South America	Sandy with dark stripes
Wild cat	5 (11)	Europe, India, Africa	Brown with black stripes

The wild cat includes the domestic cat

The life of a cat

There is an old saying that "a cat has nine lives." It is certainly true that cats are good at getting out of trouble and escaping from danger. Even so, as the cat's owner you should do all you can to protect it from harm.

A cat will live to about 15, and some live even longer. But a kitten could come to a very abrupt end if it tried testing its teeth on an electric wire! You must just train it not to do so. You must also keep all poisons out of the way. Some cats like to climb up chimneys. They can even get shut in cupboards or closets by mistake. You must also make sure that your cat does not wander into the road where there is danger from traffic.

The language of cats

Cats have moods, just as people do. Sometimes they want to be on their own to rest or sleep. At other times they want your company, and are happy just to sit near you.

▲ A kitten must be held firmly so it can't wriggle free. Use both your hands and your arms to make sure that it does not fall and hurt itself.

◀ Most pet cats enjoy human contact. If you stroke it gently, your cat will contentedly lie beside you or curl up on your knee. It will respond by purring to show its pleasure, but if its tail begins to twitch, then it is time to leave it alone as it is becoming annoyed.

When your cat wants to be stroked or petted, it may come up and brush its head against your leg. It may jump onto your lap. Some cats make a kind of chirping sound when they see their owners, rather like a human "hello." A contented cat will just sit and purr. An angry cat will twitch its tail, the opposite of a dog that does this when happy or being friendly.

You will get to know cat language in time, and your cat will get to know yours. Here are some words of warning about cats in general. However well you know your own cat, do not assume that all cats will be just as friendly. Some cats dislike being handled and they show it by biting or scratching. If a cat wants to be playful or friendly, it will come to you. Otherwise leave it alone. Sometimes cats, like humans, just want peace and quiet, so you should never disturb a sleeping cat.

▼ These two cats are not at all pleased with each other. They are about to have a fight. They arch their backs and lower their heads as a sign of anger. The tails are also lowered. Cats use their tails in a kind of body language. When they are angry, they swish their tails from side to side. A cat sometimes twitches the tip of its tail when it is very angry.

Mystery and magic

You may find that there are just a few people who do not like cats at all. They seem to have a strong feeling that cats are just a little creepy. Even though cats are mysterious animals, most people are happy to have them as family pets.

Cats in history

The first people to keep cats in the home were the ancient Egyptians. They worshiped the cat, and one of their goddesses was Pasht, a woman with a cat's head. The Egyptians believed that a cat had once saved the world by cutting off the head of a serpent that was trying to destroy the Sun!

In Europe, until about 300 years ago, cats were less popular. This was a time when people were frightened of witches. They believed that witches could turn themselves into black cats and back again. It was a bad

◄ This is known as the Alabaster Sphinx. It was built several thousand years ago at Memphis in Egypt. A sphinx was a huge statue of a woman's head on a lion's body. The ancient Egyptians had many gods and goddesses. They believed that some of them had human bodies and the heads of animals. Others, like this one, had human heads and the bodies of animals.

▲ Have you read *Alice in Wonderland* by Lewis Carroll? The Cheshire Cat was a magical animal that could vanish whenever it wanted to. When someone said "Off with its head," the cat vanished, starting with the tip of its tail and ending with the grin!

time for cats until about 1660, when a **plague** swept through Europe. This disease was caused by rats. Soon the cats became important again as they began to kill off the rats.

One group of people who understood the need for cats were America's first **settlers**. When the Pilgrim Fathers set sail in the *Mayflower*, they took some cats with them. They knew that the cats would be needed to kill the rats and mice in their grain stores.

Cats' tales

When cats became popular again, they began to appear in stories. One of the best known was *Puss·in Boots*, about a wily cat that helped its master to gain a fortune.

Cats have also been popular as cartoon characters. The first cat cartoon, *Pussyfoot*, was made in England in 1917. Then came Felix and now we have Tom and Jerry. But few real cats have appeared in films. There is no cat to compare with Lassie. This is because cats are not so easy to train as dogs are. Cats just do what they want to—they do not like doing what they are told!

▶ The musical show *Cats* is the latest example of a cat story, this time on the stage. It is based on cat poems written by T.S. Eliot, an American who spent most of his life in England. His book was called *Old Possum's Book of Practical Cats*.

Cats and their breeds

Most pet cats do not have pedigrees. This means that no one has kept a record of their parents, grandparents and earlier ancestors. Cats without pedigrees are most likely to be **crossbred**. This means they are mixtures of several **breeds**. There are many different breeds of cats.

Purebred cats have ancestors that all belonged to the same breed. In North America, about 40 breeds are recognized. In the United Kingdom, which has a different system, there are more than 100 breeds. You can read about some of the more common breeds in the next few pages.

The three main types

The breeds that pedigreed cats belong to are divided into three groups. One group contains most of the longhair breeds. Cats with short fur belong to one or the other of the two shorthair groups. These are the Domestic Shorthairs and the Oriental Shorthairs. Oriental Shorthairs are often called Foreign Shorthairs.

▲ The American Shorthair is heavily built, but is a gentle cat. It has a very loud purr, and is friendly with everyone. There are 34 recognized colors and coat patterns.

◄ The Blue Shorthair, or British Blue as it is usually called, has short legs and a powerful body. This one is a Grand Champion called Emercel Hyperian. The head is round in shape and the eyes are copper colored.

► This British Red Spotted is very similar to the Red Tabby Shorthair. These cats have large eyes and bright pink noses. The pads beneath their paws are bright pink also. We sometimes call these "Marmalade cats" because of their colors.

▼ The American Wirehair is quiet, but not quite so friendly as the American Shorthair. It has a thick, wiry coat. There are also 34 colors and patterns of Wirehair coats. Most Wirehairs have golden eyes.

Domestic Shorthairs

In Western countries, the oldest breeds with short fur are the American and British Shorthairs. Their ancestors were the mousers of Europe, brought north from Italy by the ancient Romans.

Shorthaired cats in this group have a variety of different colors, including black, white, cream, blue, tortoiseshell and tabby. These colors are found in both the American and British Shorthairs. There is a big difference between the two types. They may be the same colors but they are different shapes.

The American Shorthair is a powerful-looking, very active cat. Its neck is more noticeable than that of the British Shorthair. Most family cats in the United States are of the American Shorthair type. They are gentle and very friendly, so they fit in well with family life. The British Shorthair is larger than the American, with a heavier body and shorter legs. Most British **moggies** look like this. Most domestic shorthaired cats have smooth, sleek fur. But one American shorthaired cat is quite different. This new breed, the American Wirehair, has fur that is wiry and crinkled.

19

Foreign and Oriental Shorthairs

It is easy to recognize the Foreign and **Oriental** Shorthairs by their shape and appearance. They have lean bodies and long legs. Most of the breeds have long, whip-like tails and V-shaped faces. The best known Oriental Shorthair is the Siamese.

▼ The Siamese has long legs and a long whip-like tail. All Siamese have very bright blue eyes. They are intelligent and loyal to their owners, but can be prickly with strangers.

Red Point Siamese

The Siamese

Some of the breeds that are called Oriental first started in the United States or Europe, but the Siamese really did come from the East. There are pictures of Siamese cats in an old book of Thai poems written around 1350, so we know it is a very old Oriental breed.

A Siamese has a slender body, long legs and tail, slanting eyes and large ears. It is easily recognized by its coat pattern. It has pale fur with darker "points" on its face, ears, paws and tail. The points can be brown, blue —and in Britain, though not in the United States—red or **tabby** as well.

Seal Point Siamese

The Burmese

The Burmese breed started in 1930, when a U.S. Navy doctor called Joseph Thompson brought a little brown cat home with him from Burma. She looked like a dark Siamese, and the doctor mated her with Siamese cats to produce the first Burmese kittens.

The main Burmese coat colors are all brown or all blue. "Blue" cats are really a soft bluish-gray.

▼ The Burmese is a very athletic cat and full of fun. It has a glossy coat, with matching nose and paw pads.

▲ This fine Abyssinian cat is watching goldfish. Its coat is like rabbit fur.

▼ The coat of the Devon Rex is curly and waved. The head is V-shaped, and the eyes and ears are large.

The Abyssinian

Some people think that Abyssinians are descended from the cats once worshiped in Egypt. The first ones were brought from Africa to Europe by British soldiers in the 1860s. Their fur is ticked like that of a rabbit: each hair is banded with a darker color. This cat is sometimes called the "Bunny Cat."

The Rex

Rex cats have bodies like other cats in this group, but their coats are curly rather than straight. There are two main Rex breeds, the Cornish and the Devon. They started in neighboring counties in England. The first Devon was a kitten born to an adopted stray. A Devon Rex has a shorter nose than a Cornish Rex, and enormous ears.

The Longhairs

This group includes some of the most beautiful cats in the world. But keeping them beautiful is hard work, for they need a long grooming session every day to prevent their coats from getting tangled. If you think you might not have the time, it is best to choose a breed with short fur instead.

The most famous Longhair breed is the Persian but there are several others. The first longhaired cats to come west—in the 1500s—were the Turkish Angoras, which look like slimmer, silkier Persians.

▼ The Himalayan or Colorpoint is essentially a Persian with Siamese coloring. The main color is confined to the mask, legs and tail. The coat is long, thick, soft and silky and stands out a long way from the body. The ruff is particularly full, and extends to a frill between the front legs.

◄ This Red Tabby Persian is stepping carefully through the long grass. He has short, sturdy legs and a long, flowing coat. Persians have large heads with small ears. They are friendly and love being petted by their owners.

The Persian

The Persian is the fluffiest of all the Longhairs. Its wonderful coat feels thick and soft to the touch, and forms a big frill, or "ruff," around its neck. Under all the fur it has a solid, stocky body, with rather short legs and tail. Its nose and ears are also short, and the head is round.

▲ **This beautiful longhaired cat is a Seal Point Birman. You can recognize this breed by its four white feet, which was the sign of the Burmese temple cats. The eyes are a brilliant blue.**

▼ **The Turkish Van has a fine coat of white fur with reddish markings on the head and tail. The eyes are large and orange in color to match the markings.**

Persians have many varieties of color, with blue, black and white the most common. There are also tabby Persians and a variety called Smoke. These have dark fur with a paler **undercoat**.

Himalayan

This breed looks like a Siamese with long fur. It is really a Persian cat with dark "points" in the Siamese pattern. Like a Persian, it has a broad face, small ears and a stocky body.

Birman

The Birman looks very like the Himalayan, but its paws are white. According to legend, the very first Birman belonged to a Burmese priest called Mun-Ha. When Mun-Ha was killed by bandits, his cat lept on his body to defend it. Its paws became snow-white when they touched his white hair.

Turkish Van

One Longhair breed really seems to enjoy being in the water. It is the Turkish Van cat, just called "the Turkish" by most people. It looks like a white Angora, but it always has a red tail and red patches on its ears. The first of this breed came from around Lake Van in Turkey, where they were famous for swimming in the streams.

Cats and kittens

From the age of about six months, female cats are able to **conceive** and have kittens. When they are slightly older, **toms** will mate if they get the chance.

◄ This Burmese Blue has been spayed recently by the vet. The operation is quite painless. The scar heals up quickly and the fur starts growing again. In a few weeks this cat's fur will be back to normal again. She will be unable to have kittens, but she will be easier to look after.

Spaying and neutering

Any vet will tell you that it is best to have females **spayed** and toms **neutered**. This will prevent the female from having kittens, and the tom from mating. As a result, there will be fewer unwanted kittens. Also, a tom that has not been neutered will leave an unpleasant smell in your house. Unspayed females are noisy and sometimes smelly.

Spaying and neutering are small, painless operations. They are always done by the vet, and cats soon recover. Afterward, they are more home-loving. Outside, they are less likely to roam or to fight other cats. Spaying or neutering is usually done from the age of six months onward.

▲ This Blue Tonkinese Shorthair is pregnant. Her tummy is larger than usual because kittens are growing inside her.

▼ Soon after they are born, kittens start feeding on their mother's milk. These kittens are only a few days old and their eyes are not yet open. They are too young to be handled, and it is best to watch them from a distance.

Young kittens

It may be that you have decided to have a kitten as a pet. If so, you must wait until it is at least ten weeks old before bringing it home. Kittens are born blind and without teeth. After about a week, their eyes open. A week later they start to crawl. Soon they begin to explore, and the mother starts the job of training them. She will teach them to use the toilet tray and to come back to her if they wander away.

Kittens start life by feeding on their mother's milk. When they are between four and eight weeks old they begin to change to a diet of solid food. You can read more about feeding kittens on page 28.

Young kittens are happy with their mother, and their brothers and sisters. Remember that your kitten will be frightened when it leaves its family and comes to your home. Try to avoid sudden loud noises or movements. Keep children and other pets out of the way until your kitten settles in. When you pick it up, remember that its bones are still very **fragile**. Handle it very gently.

Your cat's new home

The day you bring your cat home is a very important day in its life—and in your life too. If you plan carefully, you can make it a good day for you and your new pet.

The first day

Choose a day when you have plenty of time to spare and when life at home is not going to be too busy. You will need to have some things ready beforehand. You will need a place for your cat to sleep and a litter tray (see page 30).

A safe home

Cats do not like changes and your cat may be frightened and unsettled. It is up to you to show it that your house is a good home. That way, it is less likely to want to escape. Decide on one room that will be the cat's base for the first day or two. This should be a room where it will not be disturbed, but where it can hear people moving and talking. Make sure that the window is shut and the door is kept closed. If there is a chimney or any other opening for the cat to explore, block it up.

▲ A cat and a dog sharing the same home soon become friends, but you must be careful during the first few days in case there are problems.

▼ You should keep a goldfish bowl or a fish tank in a place where your cat cannot go. Cats and kittens are hunters. An adventurous kitten could fall into a fish tank and might drown.

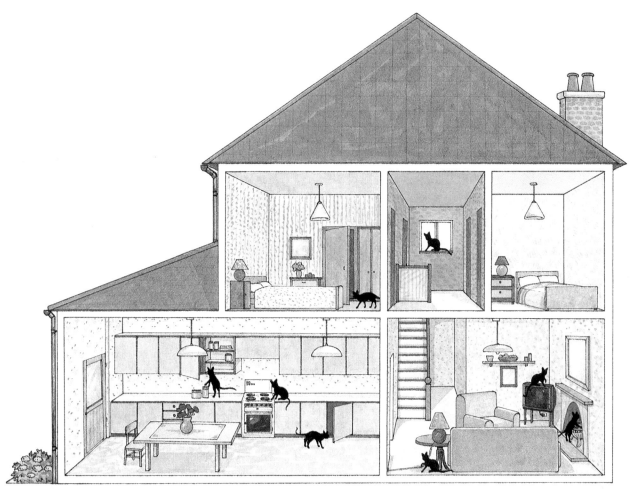

▲ There is an old saying "curiosity killed the cat!" Is your home a safe one for your pet? Here are a few useful tips for you to follow: Keep bedroom doors closed. Keep all closet doors closed. Keep low windows closed. Do not let your cat go behind the TV. Do not let your cat play with electric wires. Block up an open chimney. Keep your cat away from the stove.

It is important for your cat to realize as soon as possible that you are its owner. This is called **bonding**. Your new pet may not want to play on its first day. If it does, spend some time with it, talking quietly and using its name. Most likely it will want to sleep and settle down in its new home.

Your cat will soon be ready to explore other rooms in the house and meet other members of the family. This may include a dog or another cat. Dogs and cats that share a home will soon get on well with each other. Take care at first in case the dog is jealous of your new pet. Make sure that the dog also receives plenty of attention.

Feeding your cat

Cats are creatures of habit. They like things to happen at the same time and in the same place each day. Make sure that your cat has regular meal times and that the food dish is put down in the same place. Always place a dish of fresh water near the food dish.

Cats like a quiet place to have their food and are often slow eaters. Always clean the dish after the cat has finished. If there is some food left over, put out less food at the next meal until you have found the right amount.

Feeding kittens

Kittens need to be fed more often than adult cats because they cannot **digest** as much food at a time. Start by giving your kitten the same amount of food as it has been used to. Give it the same kind of food at the same times. It is usual to start with four meals a day. Cut back slowly to three and then to two meals a day. Increase the amounts of food at the same time.

▼ The milk bowl in this picture is too deep and sloping for the small kitten. As you can see, it is having difficulty getting its head down to drink the milk. A shallow bowl with straight sides would be much more suitable.

▲ Feed your cat at the same times. Then it will be eager for its food!

▼ This Abyssinian cat sometimes finds an extra meal by killing unwary birds! Bird baths and feeders should be placed so that hunting cats cannot reach them.

Kittens need **milk feeds**, such as soft, unsweetened breakfast cereal mixed with milk, as well as meat. As they grow up, many cats go on enjoying milk. Do not give them milk straight from the refrigerator. Let it stand for a while to take the chill off.

Feeding adult cats

Adult cats should have two meals a day—one in the morning and another in the evening. It is probably best to vary the food you give—but your cat may not let you do this. Cats are fussy eaters and some will go hungry rather than try anything new.

Most canned cat foods contain all the things needed to keep cats healthy. Many cats enjoy dry and **semi-moist** food from packages, but here is a warning. These foods must not be used unless your cat will drink water, either separately or mixed with the food. Cats should not be fed on them all the time.

A cat's place

Every cat needs a base—somewhere in the house where it feels safe and warm. Cats are sometimes fussy about where their base is. Most cats like it to be slightly raised off the floor, in a place where they can see what is going on. They like a warm spot. You can spend a lot of money on a special cat bed, but your cat will be just as happy in a cardboard box like the one in the picture.

Things you will need

Your cat will also need a litter tray. Put this in a corner out of the way so that the cat can use it without being watched. A cat that is allowed out will use the garden for its toilet, but kittens need a tray—and so, often, do old cats. You can buy special trays, but any large plastic tray will do. Put cat litter or sand in it, because cats are clean animals and like to cover up what they have done.

▲ You can make your cat box cozy by lining it with soft old clothes. Make sure that your cat's bed is placed in a warm draft-free corner with easy access to its cat tray or pet door.

▶ Cats prefer to be able to come and go as they please. You can buy a ready-made pet door from the pet shop. It should be lightweight or gently sprung so that your cat can come in and go out easily without getting its tail caught.

You will need to decide whether to let your cat go out of the house and in again as it wishes. If so, you will need a pet door on one of the outside doors. You can buy one ready-made, but you will need some help to fit it to the door. You will also have to show your cat how it works.

A cat's territory

Most cats like to lead two lives. One is indoors with its owner. The other is outdoors—hunting, tracking and watching. A cat moving to a new neighborhood will soon mark out its **territory**. It may even use the same territory as other cats, but at different times of the day. Cats work out their territory for themselves without any help from humans.

A "bird's-eye view" of cat territories.

1. A female cat has a smaller territory than a male. She fiercely defends it, especially if she has kittens. 2. Male tom cats wander farther afield, often in the yard of a house that has no cats. 3. Cats from the same house learn to share their territory. 4. Walls and outside areas are neutral territory.

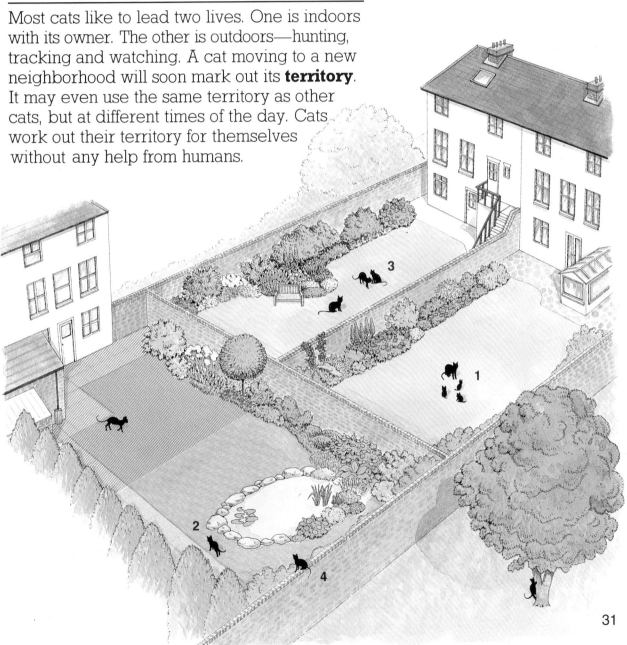

Grooming and hygiene

If you groom your kitten gently from the start, it will enjoy it. It will feel as if it is being stroked. With an older cat, this may be more difficult and you will need to be patient. Always take care when you are grooming any cat to keep your face well out of the way of its claws. All you need for grooming is a soft brush and a metal comb. Use these for your cat only and wash them often.

◀ **This Blue Point Birman (*left*), with its long coat, needs to be groomed daily. You should hold the cat firmly with one hand, and comb it with the other hand. With longhairs, grooming is best done on a table.**

▼ **Grooming a shorthair (*right*) is an easier job. You should comb away from the head and toward the tail.**

Grooming equipment

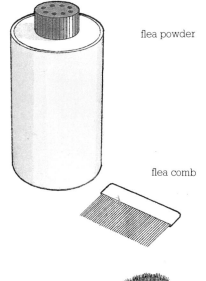

flea powder

flea comb

brush for coat

double-sided metal comb

metal comb

Grooming a shorthair

Shorthairs need less grooming than longhairs, but they should have some attention every day. Groom gently with a stroking movement. Watch carefully to make sure that you brush away any hair that comes loose. At the same time, keep an eye out for fleas.

You can buy flea powder from the pet shop. This will get rid of any fleas in the fur and keep them away for a while. Read the instructions on the package carefully. Always get someone to help you use flea powder. Some cats will struggle and need to be held firmly. You must not get any powder into the cat's eyes or mouth. Wash your hands well after using the flea powder.

Grooming a longhair

Longhairs need more lengthy grooming, every day. Their hair easily gets in a tangle. First use the comb gently to comb out any tangles. Then follow up with the brush. An old, soft toothbrush can be used gently around the face and eyes.

The secret of successful grooming is to start as soon as you can, when your kitten is quite young. Make it a part of your daily pet care. Your cat may wriggle at first, but do not give up. It will soon accept grooming as a part of daily life. It helps to speak to your cat in a gentle manner while grooming.

As well as keeping the cat's coat healthy, grooming also helps you to watch out for signs of injuries or other health problems.

Play and exercise

All cats are natural hunters. Watch young kittens at play, and you will see that all their games are to do with hunting. They learn to **stalk** their prey, to pounce on it and then kill it. They behave in the same way, whether the prey is a live mouse or a ball of paper!

Playing with your kitten

A kitten's mother teaches it the first lessons in hunting. When you bring your kitten home, you have to take her place. You can buy special toys, but a thread spool, a pingpong ball or a ball of paper on a string will do just as well. But never let a cat play with any object small enough to stick in its throat.

Many cats enjoy "hunting" inside a cave of corrugated paper, or in a large paper bag. Make sure that it is paper, not plastic. Let your pet explore before it steps inside. Otherwise the game might frighten the cat.

▲ These kittens like playing with their owner. A soft ball on the end of a string makes a good plaything.

◄ This Burmese Blue is playing a hunting game. Cats love paper bags, but you should never let them play with plastic bags. They cannot breathe through the plastic.

As cats grow older they spend less time playing, but many still enjoy a daily game with their owners. In the yard, they will find as much exercise as they want climbing trees.

Taking your cat for a walk

Being taken for a walk like a dog is something that cats find hard, but they can be trained to it. If you move to a new home, it may be a good idea to walk your cat on a leash in the yard for a few days. That way, you can show the cat its new territory.

If you decide to do this, your cat must have a cat harness. The first step is to loop a string through the harness. Let the cat get used to walking free with it indoors. Step two is to hold the end of the string and let the cat feel a gentle tug as you lead it around, still indoors. Then, you can take the cat for a short walk in the yard.

▲ All cats like climbing trees. The scratches at the foot of the tree are where the cat has been sharpening its claws.

▶ You can buy a cat harness like the one in the picture from most pet stores.

Training your pet

There are some things your cat must learn to do or not to do. Use its name often when you are training it. Encourage it to come when you call. Never hit a cat if it does something wrong. Instead, say "No" loudly and firmly.

The litter tray

Mother cats usually teach their kittens to use the litter tray, but you may have to train your kitten yourself. Provide a tray with plenty of loose litter in it. Litter from the pet shop is good, but it is expensive. Sand or earth from the yard will do just as well. Always change the litter when it has been used.

Show your cat what the tray is for by putting it gently on the litter. Using your fingers, show it how to make the litter move with its front paws. Do this several times at odd moments so that the cat gets used to the idea. At other times, if you think the cat wants to use the tray, take it there. Encourage it by talking and using its name. Choose a place for the tray away from its feeding place. It must be in a place where the cat can use it at any time.

▲ One way to teach a cat to come to you is to tap its food dish with a spoon. You can give it a treat, such as a small piece of cheese, when it comes to you. Do not tease your cat by calling it if you do not have food.

◄ Getting your cat to use the litter tray may take quite a long time, but you must go on trying. Your first task is to show the cat how to move the litter around with its front paws.

Sharp claws

A cat's claws are its hunting tools, and its instinct is to keep them sharp. If you have a yard with trees in it, your cat will probably sharpen its claws there. But many cats and kittens may try to use the furniture or carpets. The way to avoid this is to provide the cat with a scratching pad or post of its own. You could buy one, but the pictures show how to make a pad for yourself. Do not use carpet from your own house or the cat will be confused. Show your cat how to use the pad. Say "No" loudly if it tries to scratch anywhere else, and take it to the correct place.

How to make a scratching pad

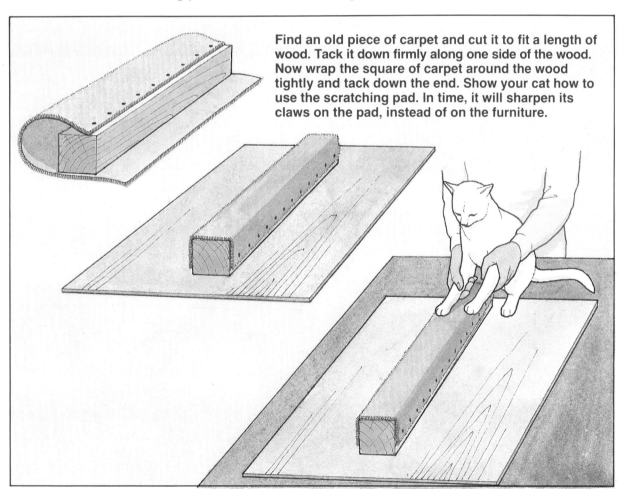

Find an old piece of carpet and cut it to fit a length of wood. Tack it down firmly along one side of the wood. Now wrap the square of carpet around the wood tightly and tack down the end. Show your cat how to use the scratching pad. In time, it will sharpen its claws on the pad, instead of on the furniture.

Keeping your cat healthy

You will soon learn how your pet looks and behaves when it is fit and well. Watch when you are grooming it for signs of poor health and for **parasites** like cat fleas. A cat cannot tell you if it does not feel well. You should watch out for changes in its mood and behavior.

Signs of illness

Many cats leave their food once in a while. If this goes on for more than one meal, it may be a sign of illness. One sure sign of ill-health is when the **haws** are showing. The haws are the grayish "third eyelids," which are normally hidden in the corners of the eyes.

Cats vomit very easily, and an occasional attack is nothing to worry about. But if vomiting persists it may be a sign of illness. Then you should ask the vet for advice. You cannot treat a cat yourself. If it is ill, take it to the vet. Never give a cat medicine intended for humans.

▲ If your cat has ear trouble, take it to the vet. He uses a special instrument to look inside the cat's ears to see what is the matter.

Giving your cat a quick health check	
Eyes	These should look clear. No sign of haws. No runny discharge. Cat should not rub its eyes with paws.
Ears	No head-shaking or ear-scratching. No brown wax in ears.
Mouth	Breath should be sweet. No dribbling. No tartar on teeth. Check teeth when cat yawns.
Fur	Fur should be thick, glossy and springy. Lank fur is often a sign of illness. Watch for dandruff, bare patches and parasites.
Mood	Should be lively and interested. Appetite should be normal. The cat should be as active as usual.
Breathing	This should be quiet and regular. There should be no heavy sneezing or coughing. Remember that some cats snore!

How to give your cat a pill

▶ 1. Open the cat's mouth gently but firmly and pop in the pill. 2. Stroke the cat's throat to help it swallow the pill.

▲ Cats often eat grass to help them digest their food. This does not matter if your cat seems fit and well.

Going to a vet

You should always take a new cat or kitten to the vet for a check-up and to have its **injections**. These will protect your cat against the most serious diseases such as distemper. A kitten can have its first injection when it is about ten weeks old. Then it will need a **booster** shot once a year. The vet will give you a card that will tell you when to take your cat in again.

Medicine for cats is usually in the form of pills. Cats do not take pills easily. You will need help from an adult if you have to give your cat pills. The trick is to hold the cat's mouth gently but firmly open, pop the pill in, and then stroke the cat's throat to help it swallow. Then watch the cat for a time. Some cats have a habit of keeping the pill in the mouth and spitting it out when they think no one is looking! The picture below may help you if you ever have to give your cat a pill.

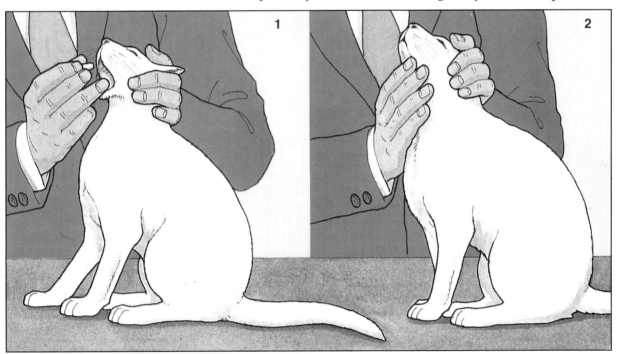

Showing your cat

There are some cat shows that have classes for family pets as well as for pedigree cats. If your cat is crossbred, but a good example of its type, you may want to show it in the future. You will need to go to a number of cat shows first to find out what happens.

About cat shows

Cat shows throughout the world differ in the way they are run. In Britain and most Commonwealth countries, cats are judged in their cages. Owners and members of the public are not allowed at the judging. In most North American shows, they are shown and judged in the judging ring.

In all cat shows there are strict rules about what may be put in the cat's cage. Each cat is checked by a vet before it is allowed in.

Cat show associations use different systems of judging. Some award points for different features of a cat's appearance. Other associations judge by a cat's general appearance. The cat show associations publish their rules so that you can see what the judges are looking for. In the United States, the judges use a points system.

▲ In 1871, a cat fancier called Harrison Weir, decided to run a cat show at Crystal Palace in London. This old print shows some of the strange-looking prizewinners. This was one of the first cat shows in the world.

◄ This beautiful cat received these cups and became Supreme Champion when he was only 6½ months old. He is a type of Chinchilla, which have coats that are very lightly tipped with a contrasting color.

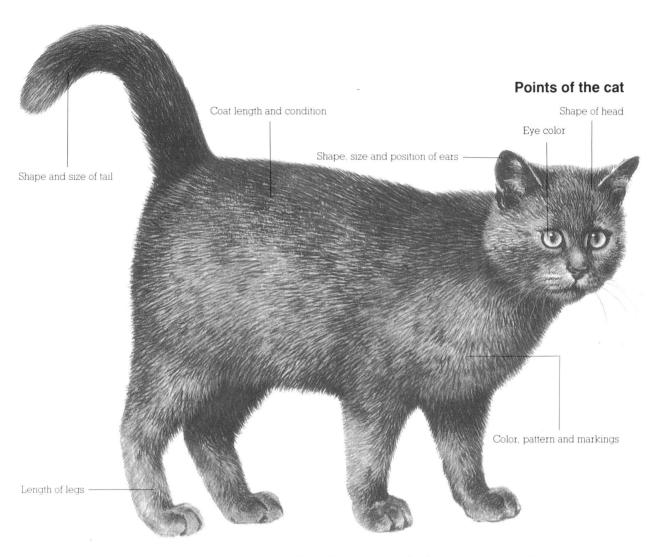

Points of the cat

Shape of head

Eye color

Coat length and condition

Shape, size and position of ears

Shape and size of tail

Color, pattern and markings

Length of legs

▲ **For a show cat to become a champion, it must look healthy and alert and the right shape and size for the breed. Each breed has a standard, and the show cat must meet all the points laid down for the breed. If it falls short and fails to make the grade in any of these points, marks are taken off. This picture shows the main points of the cat.**

Cat show associations, such as the International Cat Association in the U.S., lay down standards for each breed. These say exactly what a perfect example of each breed and variety should look like. In Britain, the rules of cat shows are laid down by the Governing Council of the Cat Fancy (GCFF).

Preparing a cat for showing means hours of hard work. Some of the books listed on page 45 will tell about the special grooming and other preparations that are needed. The best way to pick up more tips is to go to as many shows as you can. See the prize-winning owners and their cats, and if possible talk to some of the owners.

Cats of all kinds

In this book you have met just a few of the many different varieties of cats. On these pages are some more for you to look for. You may not be able to see all the types there are, even at a large cat show.

Balinese

The Balinese is a Siamese with long fur. Underneath its silky coat, this breed has the long legs and tail, the big ears and the pointed face of a typical Foreign Shorthair. Also, like the Siamese, it has blue eyes.

Chartreux

The Chartreux is a beautiful blue Domestic Shorthair that first came from France. It looks rather like the British Blue, but its blue-gray color is a little more silvery. It has gold or copper-colored eyes, and a pleased expression on its face.

Cymric

The Cymric—the name comes from the Welsh for "Wales"—is a longhaired cat with no tail. Its ancestors were Manx cats that happened to be born with long fur. Like a Manx, it has long hind legs.

▲ The longhaired Maine Coon is a non-pedigreed large domestic cat found in Maine. It is a good family cat, friendly, and with a very quiet, squeaky voice. Maine Coons come in a wide variety of colors.

◄ Manx cats have no tails and a large, stocky rump. They are not good cats for beginners as many of them suffer from weak spines.

Ragdoll

The Ragdoll is a new breed not yet recognized everywhere. There are three color varieties: one looks like a big Birman, and another like a big Himalayan. The third also looks like a Himalayan, but has a lot of white on its body. The Ragdoll is very docile and gentle. It loves being handled and that is how it got its name.

► The Scottish Fold has ears that are folded downward. This makes them look like small dogs and they are easy to recognize. They make very good pets and are friendly to everyone. Some of these cats suffer from ear trouble.

Scottish Fold

The Scottish Fold is easily recognized because its ears fold over rather than standing upright. People often say that it looks like a small dog. The breed started by accident when a kitten with folded ears was born on a farm in Scotland.

"Si-Rex"

Siamese markings—the dark ears, face, paws and tail—have been transferred to cats in several other breeds. In the "Si-Rex," the markings have been bred into the Rex cat. The result is a curly-coated cat with points of dark brown, blue or several other colors.

▼ This Turkish Angora is a champion. It has a beautiful coat and large, wistful eyes. With its long white coat it will need a lot of careful grooming.

Glossary

adult: an animal that is fully grown

bonding: the understanding between a pet and its owner

booster: a further dose or injection after a period of time to give your pet continued protection against a disease

breed: a kind or class of animal having parents of the same kind. Each breed of animal can be recognized by its size, coat, color, etc.

breeder: a person who keeps animals so as to produce young from them

canine tooth: a long, sharp tooth for holding prey and tearing off meat

carnivore: a flesh-eating animal

conceive: to become pregnant with young

crossbred: born of parents of more than one breed

digest: to break down food inside the body so that it can be used for growth and energy

domestic: describes an animal that is not wild, and is kept in the home or on a farm

fragile: easily broken

groom: to brush and comb the fur

haws: the "third eyelids," which show when a cat is unwell

injections: shots given by a vet to protect your cat against illnesses

instinct: natural behavior that does not have to be learned

litter: (1) the young kittens resulting from one mating (2) sawdust or other material used in a toilet tray

milk feed: a meal made up of milk and cereal

moggy: a British name for a mixed-breed domestic cat

neutering: an operation by the vet on a tom cat so that it cannot mate

Oriental: coming from Asia and Eastern countries

parasites: insects such as fleas that live on an animal's coat

pedigreed: having ancestors of the same breed

plague: a deadly disease

pupil: the hole in the central colored part of the eye. In cats, the pupil is seen as a slit by day, and opens wide at night

semi-moist: a type of cat food bought in packages

settler: a person who goes from one country to live in another country

spaying: an operation by the vet on a female cat so that it cannot breed

stalk: to follow prey without being seen

tabby: a cat with dark bands and markings on its fur

territory: the area in which an animal lives and hunts

tom: a male cat that has not been neutered

undercoat: the soft part of a cat's coat closest to the skin

Further reading

Caring For Your Cat by Mark McPherson. Troll Associates, 1985.
The Cat You Care For by Felicia Ames. New American Library, 1968.
How We Got Our First Cats by Tobi Tobias. Franklin Watts, 1980.
My First Kitten by Rosemarie Hauslierr. Four Winds Press, 1985.
Perfect Name for Your Pet by Texe and Wanda Marrs. Heian International Publishing, Inc., 1983.
Pets by Leda Blumberg. Franklin Watts, 1983.
Things to Know Before You Get a Pet by Lisa Marsoli. Silver, 1985.
Understanding Your Cat by Michael Fox. Bantam Books, 1977.
Your First Pet and How to Take Care of It by Carla Stevens. MacMillan, 1974.

Cat magazines

All Cats
Cats Magazine
Cat World
CFA Yearbook

Useful addresses

American Cat Association, 10065 Foothill Boulevard, Lakeview Terrace, California 91342
American Cat Fanciers Association, PO Box 203, Point Lookout, Missouri 65726
American Humane Association, 5351 South Roslyn Street, Englewood, Colorado 80111
American Society for the Prevention of Cruelty to Animals, 441 East 92nd Street, New York, New York 10028
Cat Fanciers Association, 1309 Allaire Avenue, Ocean, New Jersey 07712
Cat Fanciers Federation, 4106 Muhammad Ali Boulevard, Louisville, Kentucky 40212
United Cat Federation, 6616 East Hereford Drive, Los Angeles, California 90022

Index